SWATI SENGUPTA is an author and journalist. Her books include *Out of War* (Speaking Tiger Books, 2016), *Guns on My Red Earth* (Rupa, 2013), *Half the Field Is Mine* (Scholastic, 2014), *The Talking Bird* (Tulika Books, 2014) and *A Tea Garden Party* (Pratham Books, 2021). She translated *Murder in the City* (Speaking Tiger Books, 2018) from Bengali to English. Swati runs a workshop series on gender for young adults. She studied English at Jadavpur University and lives in Kolkata.

Also in the series by Swati Sengupta:

*Jhalkari Bai: The Braveheart Warrior*

*Milkha Singh: The Runner Who Could Fly*

*Birsa Munda: The Great Revolutionary Leader*

# The Incredible Life of Savitribai Phule

## The Fearless Reformer

Swati Sengupta

Illustrations by Devashish Verma

An Imprint of Speaking Tiger Books

TALKING CUB

Published by Speaking Tiger Books LLP
125A, Ground Floor, Shahpur Jat,
Near Asiad Village, New Delhi 110 049

First published in paperback in Talking Cub
by Speaking Tiger Books in 2023

Text copyright © Swati Sengupta 2023

Illustration copyright © Speaking Tiger Books 2023

ISBN: 978-93-5447-420-0

eISBN: 978-93-5447-443-9

10 9 8 7 6 5 4 3 2 1

Typeset in Georgia by Jojy Philip
Printed at Shree Maitrey Printech Pvt. Ltd., Noida

No part of this publication may be reproduced, transmitted, or stored in a retrieval system, in any form or by any means, electronic, mechanical, photocopying, recording or otherwise, without the prior permission of the publisher.

This book is sold subject to the condition that it shall not, by way of trade or otherwise, be lent, resold, hired out, or otherwise circulated, without the publisher's prior consent, in any form of binding or cover other than that in which it is published.

For Riddho,

because he knows how important 'equality' is.

## Chapter One

Everyone was asking her to smile. They said her smile was beautiful. The kohl that had been rubbed on her eyes made them itch and water. She sat there quietly, sad and uncomfortable. Her eyes filled with tears often—was it because of the kohl, or was it for some other reason?

All around her festivities swirled. There was the earthy smell of marigold flowers, laddoos were piled up in one place, colourful decorations had turned their house so beautiful. Her friends were all giddy with excitement. But Savitri sat alone, not saying much.

Someone came and placed a bindi on her forehead. She was made to wear a heavy sari. Pieces of jewellery were slipped on her small body. She felt she was carrying the weight of the world—it was too much for this nine year old.

The year was 1840, and this was Savitri's wedding day. She had no idea what 'getting married' meant. Her mind was filled with so many worries. What if her 'new family' disliked her? She was anxious, and she really wanted to cry. Savitri knew of many girls who had been married when they were even younger than her. Sometimes, when their husbands, who were much older, died, their long hair got chopped off or shaved off. They were not allowed to play with their friends any more. They were not allowed to read or write. They had to live separately.

*Savitri did not want to be like that.*

But where she was born–in Naigaon of Maharashtra's Satara–most girls were married off young. Some to men who were much older, and if the man died, the girls lived miserable lives forever. No one got away.

> Child marriage was rampant in India in the early 19th century. Most of the country by now was under the direct or indirect control of the British. The Bengal Sati Regulation (a law introduced in 1829 that made the practice of Sati illegal and punishable) and the Hindu Widows' Remarriage Act of 1856 were two important laws passed in India by the British to stop violence against women. Through the latter, widows were supported by law when they decided to marry again. But it took many years for people to actually 'accept' these laws in favour of women.

Lakshmi and Khandoji Nevase Patil, Savitri's parents, were happy that their daughter was getting married to a good person. 'He will make you very happy, Savitri,' her mother said, gently stroking her head. The groom they had chosen was Jyotirao Phule. He was thirteen years old and his family owned some farmland. He had even studied in school.

But Savitri did not know this Jyotirao, the thirteen-year-old boy, at all. Was he happy to be married? Savitri had no idea and she didn't care.

Marriage was ruining her life. Soon, she would have to cook and clean in the new home. She would be expected to have children. She would never be a knowledgeable person, Savitri felt as she sat sorrowfully on her wedding day, surrounded by her friends, family and neighbours.

Little did Savitri know that none of her fears would come true. Her life was going to be very different from that of other women. And one day, she would bring enormous changes in the lives of thousands of others.

Jyotirao was kind, gentle and a deep thinker. He never accepted customs, rules and regulations unless he could justify them with his own reasoning. He had gone to school because he had been keen to learn. That's the first thing Savitri liked about him.

Soon, Savitri went to his home in Poona (or Pune), which was so far from her own home in Naigaon it made her want to cry. She missed her parents so much. But Jyotirao understood her pain and tried his best to make her feel comfortable. He brought her food she liked, and said funny things to try to make her smile. He felt sorry she had to leave her parents' home to live with him and his family, whom she did not know at all. He was also sorry that Savitri, like most women, was not allowed to study in school. This girl whom he had married, seemed bright and gritty. She was not easy to please and had a mind of her own. That's exactly what he wanted. This was a person who could be his friend.

Jyotirao had lost his mother when he was only a year old, and had been brought up by his father's cousin, Sagunabai Kshirsagar. She was a child widow who worked with a Christian missionary that looked after orphans.

At this time, access to education was mostly monopolized by brahmins—one of the so-called upper caste groups. Jyotirao's father, Govindrao, had never gone to school himself, and wanted his son to get a formal education. Govindrao admitted Jyotirao to a school. However, as Jyotirao grew older, he faced numerous discriminations and opposition. This was because, like Savitri, Jyotirao, too, was a shudra—one of the so-called lower caste groups in the caste system that plagued Indian society, and shudras were barred from getting formal education. A brahmin clerk did not like a shudra studying there and Govindrao was forced to take his son out of school.

So here was a strong-minded Savitri who never got the opportunity to study. And here was Jyotirao who had felt humiliated when he was deprived of a school education for being a shudra. She was a shudra woman—which meant she had to endure double the obstacles he faced.

A sensitive man like Jyotirao Phule understood Savitri's pain. They were both considered weak and denied equal opportunities. But the good thing was that both refused to accept their condition.

In no time, Savitri lost her apprehensions about Jyotirao. They became friends very easily and grew fond of each other. There was a lot of respect on both sides. This love and respect only grew stronger over the years. Savitri had been married so young that her life almost started with Jyotirao.

This is where this story begins: with a marriage that was like a journey—one that would bring about a sweeping social revolution touching the lives of countless Indians in the days ahead.

Jyotirao could not accept being left out of school. He was restless and desperate to learn, so he kept reading and writing all the time! Scholar Gaffar Baig Munshi and a British official Lizit Sahab—both known to Jyotirao—were impressed by how his heart ached. Gaffar Baig Munshi was a Persian scholar. Lizit Sahab was a Christian, and they both believed in the importance of education. They explained to Govindrao what a significant change it could bring to his child's life and persuaded him to admit Jyotirao to school again.

In 1841, Baig and Lizit Sahab helped the young man get admission in a missionary school. Lizit Sahab told Jyotirao's father that brahmins often advised shudras to not send their children to missionary schools. The missionaries would convert their children to Christianity, was what they said. However, this seemed to be a ploy to keep shudras out of school education, which the brahmins wanted to control. They themselves sent their children to school, so they obviously understood the importance of formal education.

What would brahmins gain in preventing shudras from going to school? Why did they claim to be superior? Why and how did they control the education system? Many of these answers lie in India's ancient caste/varna system.

In the varna system, Hindu society is divided into four varnas (classes): brahmins, kshatriyas, vaishyas and shudras. Those who are outside these four groups were called the avarna.

A book called *Manusmriti* (The Laws of Manu), that dates back to more than 1,000 years before the birth of Christ, is said to acknowledge and justify the caste system as the basis of order in society. It is also believed that these four groups were created from Brahma, the Hindu god of creation.

At the top were the brahmins, said to have come from Brahma's head. They were the intellectuals, teachers, priests and scholars in society.

The kshatriyas were believed to have been born from Brahma's arms. They were the rulers, warriors and administrators. The vaishyas, said to be born from the god's thighs, were the traders and merchants or those who owned land and pursued agriculture. And there were the shudras, said to be born from Brahma's feet and were labourers who worked for others.

These four main castes were further divided into various castes and sub-castes depending on people's occupations. Those who were outside the caste system were known as avarnas, or ati-shudras. Shudras and ati-shudras have faced various forms of discrimination over the ages. They were repressed and denied jobs, education and any means through which they could improve their lives. There exist many scholarly interpretations of the four-fold caste system. While some talk of society being divided on the basis of occupation, others look at it from the point of view of race, religion, regional specifications and so on.

During the British rule in India, much importance was given to *Manusmriti*, and it was translated to English. Texts like this prescribed different forms of violence to keep the social hierarchies intact. They denied shudras and ati-shudras all avenues for improving their lives, as education, or many kinds of jobs, were denied to them.

One must remember, that the British rulers were influenced by the opinions of influential and powerful people, and they were mainly Sanskrit-educated, so-called upper caste men.

This is where the story of Savitribai Phule unfolds: at a time of divisions in society into various groups and sub-groups; when caste and class were considered important, and the British were ruling over India.

Centuries of discrimination had become a way of life. Women, shudras and ati-shudras were, among other things, deprived of a school education. They had no equal rights. Would things ever change?

# *Chapter Two*

It was a beautiful morning. Savitri had now been living in her new home for some time. She looked out of the window and watched wisps of white clouds floating in the sky. Jyotirao had gone to school, and would be back only in the late afternoon. Savitri had got to know him a bit better now, and liked him. But she also enjoyed this time when he was away from home.

Some sparrows swooped down on the courtyard. They made a lot of noise as they pecked at grains, chattered amongst themselves and then flew away. They hopped about near

Savitri's window, peeping in. But she hardly paid any attention to the birds.

Her eyes were focused on Jyotirao's books and notebooks that were neatly arranged on the shelves. When he was away, Savitri took them down and pretended to read. She liked the idea of reading, even if she could not actually read or write. She liked to imagine herself as a great scholar, teacher or poet. The musty smell of old books filled her with happiness. She did not know how to read the words printed on the page in bold, black colour. She gaped at their wondrous beauty. Who knew what they were trying to tell her! What stories lay hidden within the words? What deep, philosophical thoughts may be hiding within those pages? If only she had the key to unlock the mystery!

She opened her husband's notebooks. Page after page was covered in his neat handwriting.

Even without knowing their meaning, Savitri wondered what brilliant ideas and bold expressions lay bare there. A sudden sorrow swept over her. She was exasperated. How could she not decipher what was written? Why should it be a secret?

Savitri knew from the squawking of the birds outside her window if they were happy or sad. The rustle of leaves in the wind told her stories of approaching storms. The sound of dead leaves crackling under someone's feet meant someone was approaching. The sound of rivers gurgling, the buzz of bees among the flowers—she could untangle and interpret the complexities of various sounds. Why then should words remain secret? Why did she have no access to words which floated on the pages of books? Why could she not know what they meant?

Just then, a breeze swept through the room. Raindrops came pattering down. Savitri sat by the window with a book in hand and sobbed bitterly. She hoped no one saw her crying. She did not like anyone to think that she wasn't strong. She had to find a way to learn letters.

Her heart skipped a beat when, after a few days, Jyotirao asked her if she would like to learn to read and write. He did not want his wife to suffer silently. 'Never bow down before anyone,' he said, as he promised to teach her.

He must have seen her sobbing that day! Savitri's eyes filled with tears, and yet she was dying to break into a laughter that everyone on earth could hear. How happy she was!

Eyes downcast, and shuffling her feet, she nodded.

Learning to read and write was magical. Sights, sounds, smells, and every emotion could be depicted in letters and words. There were so many ways of expressing feelings and thoughts, in so many different languages! Words could even dwell silently and patiently for years within the pages of books, waiting for someone to read them!

Stories helped the reader to fly off to distant, unknown lands. Every emotion and feeling, reason and logic, science and philosophy, treatises on revolution and freedom could be embedded in a sea of words. Only those who had the key could unearth this knowledge, and those who did not know how to read would never be able to unravel them.

Savitri now understood why the brahmins deprived the shudras, ati-shudras and women from learning. On learning about the feats and achievements of downtrodden people in other parts of the world, those in India would aspire to do the same. They too would want to bring in changes and right so many wrongs. Depriving them of knowledge would keep them silent and they would never question the wrongs being done to them.

Books gave strength and ideas. Knowledge was power!

Once she had learned to read and write, Savitri started devouring everything she could lay her hands on. She read poetry, stories, history, news and religious texts. She studied science, mathematics, politics and literature. She learnt about art, about wars, and about the history of the country.

Studying was hard work. For the next few years, Savitri did not just learn letters and words. She took lessons at home for advanced learning in different subjects. Apart from her husband Jyotirao, she also took lessons from his friends Sakharam Yeshwant Paranjpe and Keshav Shivram Bhavalkar.

Shivram Bhavalkar was a teacher. Jyotirao had many friends who wanted to fight the injustices like he did.

Once Savitri got immersed in books, she started seeing the world around her with fresh eyes. Her own real-life experiences were just as important, she understood. She saw that women her age and even younger were being married off and pushed into a life of drudgery. Why should they be denied their rights, she wondered. Why should they not go to school and get an education?

Jyotirao felt the same. He read all the time. Whatever he learned, he would discuss with Savitri every day. In this way, some years passed by. Savitri and Jyotirao got closer and thought similarly about many things.

'All girls *must* get the opportunity to study in schools,' Savitri would often say, pacing up and down the room, restless. 'But how? Haven't we been talking about it for years? Nothing has changed. Society remains as harsh and unfair to women as it was when we got married,' she told Jyotirao, exasperated. For ati-shudra women, the plight was far worse.

'If we want things to change, we must do it ourselves,' she and Jyotirao said together. They inspired each other in every possible way.

Jyotirao and Savitri both felt that Savitri could teach other girls and share her knowledge and education so that they, too, could know all the things she knew and could be in command of their lives. But she had been educated at home. She could not be a teacher without training.

So it was decided that Savitri would get formally trained as a teacher. She enrolled for a teachers' training course at an institute run by an American missionary, Cynthia Farrar. It was in Ahmednagar, which was about 120 kilometres from Pune. Farrar had come to India from Boston, and ran her mission first from Mumbai (then Bombay) from 1827. Despite the initial resistance to send girls to schools, 400 Indian girls studied at Farrar's schools by 1829. In 1839, Farrar began her work in Ahmednagar. Savitri trained as a teacher in two schools. The other was the Normal Female School in Pune run by Ms Mitchell, who was its director.

> Jyotiba Phule had some brahmin friends who assisted him and Savitribai in their work. Sadashiv Ballal Govande worked in the Judges office at Ahmednagar. One day, he and Jyotiba visited Cynthia Farrar's school for girls in Ahmednagar. They regretted that there wasn't any such school led by Indians. Later, Govande took Savitribai to Ahmednagar to train as a teacher at Ms Farrar's school.

> Keshav Shivram Bhavalkar, another friend, took up the responsibility of educating Savitribai. Sakharam Yeshwant Paranjpe, who was a social reformer, also helped in this. Once Savitribai and Jyotiba started their schools, Bhavalkar made sure girls from various places enrolled there and he also taught there.

Just a few years after that day she wept holding Jyotirao's books, wanting to read them, Savitribai Phule was a different person. She was a keen learner who had taken lessons in various subjects and received formal training as a teacher. What could stop her now from fulfilling her dreams?

'I have lived in darkness for being unlettered. How gloomy and suffocating it was to not know how to read and write,' she often told Jyotirao.

'A whole new world has now opened before me. I want to emancipate others in the same way. I can't wait to start teaching!'

In 1846, in Pune's Maharwada ('untouchables' colony'), Savitri, along with Sagunabai, Jyotirao's aunt, began to teach some girls. In turn, every day, Savitri and Sagunabai learnt something new from these girls. They heard about their lives and Savitri's heart often ached at the problems they faced. She wanted to do more. Some of them didn't want to be married as it would mean the end of these classes. Whatever difficulties they faced, they made sure to come to school to learn, determined to change their lives to some extent.

Savitri and Sagunabai encouraged them. This intense urge to study would make their lives different for sure. 'Read and write. Write about the innermost thoughts in your mind. Don't let them remain embedded in your sorrow. Set them free,' Savitri would tell the girls.

This first-hand experience of teaching the girls made Savitri ambitious. She wanted to touch the lives of more girls. This laid the foundation for something bigger and even more momentous that would take place in the days ahead.

# *Chapter Three*

By the time Savitribai Phule was a young woman of seventeen and her husband Jyotirao Phule (also known as Jyotiba Phule) was twenty-one years old, they were brainstorming, arguing, agreeing and disagreeing all the time. They talked about how the lives of those considered lesser or lower in the social order could be changed.

During one such discussion, the couple decided to open a school where girls from all castes could study. Once the decision had been made, there was so much work to be done! They had to figure out where the school could be set up. It required a house with some rooms. They needed money to buy mats, slates, chalks, books, and so many other things. But most of all, they needed girls to come to the school—girls interested in pursuing education. For only then would it be a proper school.

After months of planning, in 1848, the school opened at a house in Budhwar Peth at Tatyarao Bhide's Bhide Wada. It was the first school for women in India that was started by Indians.

In less than ten years since her marriage, Savitribai Phule had turned from an unlettered child bride to a teacher, and set up India's first school for girls to be started by Indians. Dates on the opening of the school varies, with some sources mentioning it as 1851, while many have recorded it as 1846 or 1848.

The school building was a traditional Pune house originally built in the 18th century. It dated from the time the city was the capital of the Peshwas. Wadas were typically built in two storeys in a rectangular layout with two central courtyards. These usually had eight rooms that were used by large families.

Jyotirao and Savitribai were taking a revolutionary step in giving shudra and ati-shudra women the right to learn. This was in direct opposition to much that was happening in society. However, not only did their own community encourage them, but also some of Jyotirao's friends. The house where the school started belonged to one such friend. Savitribai Phule became a teacher at Bhide Wada and there were nine girls in this school when it started.

What was going to be taught in such a school?

Here too, the Phules made a difference. They decided that the curriculum would be different from what was taught by brahmin teachers in their schools. Savitribai's school had subjects like mathematics, science and social studies instead of texts like Vedas and shastras.

> Formal schooling for girls in the Bombay Presidency region was started by the American Board of Commissioners for Foreign Missions, one of the first American Christian missionary organizations. It started a school in Bombay in 1824, and in two years, there were nine schools with an average of 340 students.
>
> Over the next ten years, along with them, the Church Missionary Society and Scottish Missionary Society also opened girls' schools in Bombay, Nashik, Ahmednagar, Thane and Bassein (Vasai).

> Some Bombay educationists and affluent shetias (the mercantile community) came together and opened some schools for girls in 1849 under the Students' Literary and Scientific Society. The Hindu College of Pune (or Poona Sanskrit College) was opened in 1821 by William Chaplin, British Commissioner in the Deccan, under the patronage of Peshwa Bajirao II's Dakshina Fund. The college was open 'for brahmins only'.
>
> The earliest school for girls opened by Indians was started by Savitribai and Jyotirao Phule in 1848.

It was obvious that Savitribai and Jyotirao's initiative would be met with stiff opposition, as we shall soon find out.

Savitri would always wake up at the crack of dawn. From the moment she opened her eyes in the morning, she would be filled with excitement for the day of teaching in school. How she marvelled at the faces of her students. They came eager to learn and with hopes of a bright future! She would not disappoint them. This school and this work were her dream come true!

After waking up, Savitri would clean the house, take a bath, cook, and get dressed to leave home. She would dress in a simple saree, always wear her mangalsutra and put a large kunku (vermillion mark) on her forehead. She would cover her head with the loose end of the saree. There! She would be ready for the day—a picture of simplicity and grace, oozing confidence.

One day, wearing a peach saree with a thin

green border, her books in a cloth bag slung on the right shoulder, Savitri headed towards Bhide Wada. It was just a few weeks since the school had opened and many parents had shown interest in enrolling their daughters.

But as she walked, loud, jeering voices came to her from all sides.

'There goes the educated woman!' someone said in a voice dripping with hatred and sarcasm.

'She will ruin our society!' said another, full of bitterness.

'What is her husband doing? Does he have no control over her?'

'Control? On the contrary, he is dancing to her tune! How can a man do that?'

'A school for shudras and ati-shudras? If they go to school, who will clean the roads and toilets?

Never imagined we would live to see this day!'

'Soon these women will wear men's clothes and send the men to the kitchen. That's what these women want. Education is ruining them, and they are ruining our society!'

'Who are the demons that gave birth to a girl like that!'

The voices were of men and women alike. Savitri's face turned red. The insults and hateful remarks hit her like a thousand poisonous arrows. Those who have fire in their belly do not necessarily seethe with anger when the world turns against them. Savitri had a cool exterior.

She knew what she was doing was like stirring up a hornet's nest and there was going to be trouble. She would have to handle this with tact. She decided to ignore the comments and walk on.

'Walk on, Savitri, don't stop,' she told herself. 'Don't let them stop you.'

Then, out of nowhere, something sticky and wet hit her. It stuck to her saree, and gave out a foul smell. Was it mud? Or was it dung? Savitri stopped dead in her tracks for a few seconds, closed her eyes and even before anyone could have noticed that she had stopped, started walking again.

'Do not hasten or reduce the pace, Savitri,' her mind directed her. 'They should not think the attack has made any difference.' She walked on. Now a stone came hurtling at her. It hit her leg but did not injure her. The pleats of her saree had protected her. Savitri marched on. She was finally at the doors of Bhide Wada. The pulsating rhythm of her heart was beating in her ears, her throat was soaked dry and a lump of sorrow stuck there. Her eyes filled with tears, but she breathed in and let her eyes dry before she entered the school. She wouldn't let it affect her.

The students and other teachers were deeply

worried at this assault on Savitribai. But she herself was calm. 'We should be happy,' she said, grinning. The others were confused.

'It shows that we are on the right path. People want to stop us because our work will crush the unfair system,' Savitri said. She went to the tap and cleaned the muck. Now that she had washed away her fears, she felt more worried about the saree. It was a gift from her mother, and she didn't have many sarees. Hers was a frugal life and whatever resources she had were to be used for the benefit of others.

The true meaning of revolution is change—a massive, long-lasting change. But 'revolution' doesn't necessarily take place through violence or by a quick transfer of power. A small step can also make a major difference.

Savitribai's school was set to bring such a change. And Savitri was right when she said they were being attacked because they were on the right track. A similar attack took place the following day, and the day after that. Savitri wondered what she should do. The few sarees she had were all getting splotches of dark stains. It was difficult to teach students all day in a soiled saree.

What should she do?

Savitri came up with a quick solution. She was practical, and always thought of dealing with difficulties through solutions rather than brooding over them. She decided to carry a spare saree in her bag, along with the books. She reached the school, changed into the freshly washed saree and packed the stained one in her bag. Sometimes, while returning home, lumps of mud were flung at her all over again, and her saree got stained. On returning home, she sometimes washed one stained saree and sometimes two.

Those who attacked her hoping to 'teach her a lesson' were confused.

'Why does she not *react*?' they wondered.

'Why does she not even stop for a moment?'

'Does she never get angry or hurt?'

'Why does she not cry out in anger or frustration?'

'Maybe she won't be back tomorrow?'

But she was seen heading towards the school the following day. And the day after that. The purpose of the attackers seemed to be getting defeated. But they would not give up. Neither would Savitribai. Every day, she would leave home with sarees in her bag, change in school, teach throughout the day, return home and wash the sarees.

The attackers found this more and more curious and frustrating. And then, she *did* react. But not in the way the attackers had expected she would.

One day, she stopped as a few balls of mud came and hit her all over again. The onlookers waited with bated breath. Perhaps she would sit on the ground and accept defeat? Maybe she would cry and admit that she had done what women should never do? Women had no right to study in schools. Maybe she would agree that she had taken a wrong path, they felt. They wanted to know what she was about to say but they were also afraid to hear what she might utter. With those calm yet piercing eyes and the confident demeanour, nothing seemed to touch her.

Savitribai said: 'As I do the sacred task of teaching my fellow sisters, the stones or cow dung that you throw seem like flowers to me. May god bless you!'

Her attackers were shell-shocked! They had expected anger and tears, not good wishes. It is not clear whether the attack on Savitribai stopped immediately after this episode. But what did happen is that despite all the attempts to stop her, the school became hugely popular. The students enjoyed studying science, literature, mathematics and social sciences. Though it had started with less than ten students, the number increased.

But soon there was yet another stiff opposition that came her way. And this time, it wasn't from strangers. The disapproval came from home.

# *Chapter Four*

People had started talking about the work Savitribai and Jyotirao Phule were doing. As a shudra woman, Savitribai was trying to upset the peace of society and its established ways, they said.

Every time Jyotirao's father, Govindrao left home, people would advise him on his 'rebellious' son and daughter-in-law. Every time a relative, friend or neighbour dropped by their home, he would be asked to rein in Savitribai and Jyotiba, or be prepared to face 'the consequences'.

Govindrao was threatened with boycott, he was ridiculed and insulted. 'We have known you for decades. You should be firm with your son and daughter-in-law, otherwise they will bring disgrace upon all of us,' they told him. 'You are not a bad man, but your son and daughter-in-law are too revolutionary for their own good,' they warned.

"Do they think everyone is equal? Do they think a brahmin and shudra can ever be equal? Do they think women and men should sit side by side and go to school, college and offices? Who will take care of the homes then?' they questioned.

'This will ruin our society, Govindrao. Do something, else this will not have a happy ending,' they threatened. Govindrao had no answer. And he couldn't take it anymore.

One evening, he summoned Jyotirao. Even before his father said anything, Jyotirao knew it was about the school. Eyes moistened, voice trembling, Govindrao told his son in no uncertain terms: 'Either you peacefully become part of the community by giving up the path you have taken, or, I have to ask you to leave my house.'

Jyotirao's heart was filled with sorrow, but he also understood his father's pain. Govindrao was powerless in the face of the threats. But neither Savitribai nor Jyotirao could give up their chosen path.

Like those splotches of dung and stones that had hit her like poisonous arrows, this rejection from her father-in-law was a big blow for Savitri. 'If our very own don't understand us, how will those strangers follow this path?' Savitri said, as

Jyotirao listened in silence, tears rolling down his cheeks. She wiped his tears. 'We have to be stronger than ever before,' he said, clearing his throat.

It was time to leave home.

But it was not an easy thing to do. Where would they go? It was not just about renting a house and all the additional expense. It was about finding a place where the couple would be left in peace to do their work. They had not earned anything from the school. Savitri didn't take a salary for teaching in Bhide Wada. For a while, they did not know what to do.

But soon there came a solution, bringing with it a glimmer of hope for the future as well. It was 1849, just a year after the Bhide Wada school was opened. One of Jyotirao's friends,

Usman Sheikh, welcomed Savitri and Jyotiba to his home.

Usman Sheikh had a sister named Fatima Sheikh. She was a gritty teenager, motivated like Savitri to pursue education.

> Savitri and Fatima were born in the same year—1831—just six days apart. Savitri's friendship with Fatima grew ever stronger over the years. Fatima was a Muslim, a religion with many hardliners as well. There were people who did not believe in education for women. Fatima had to fight social stigma and hardships to train as an educator and teach Muslim girls. She is widely considered to be the first woman Muslim teacher of India. She was one of Savitribai and Jyotirao's schools' greatest supporters and gave her time and patiently taught the students there.

The first school at Bhide Wada had closed down for some time. There was the lack of funds, as well as opposition from some people. But after some time, it reopened at Peeth Joon Gunj at a house provided by Jyotirao Phule's friend Sadashiv Ballal Govande. He also provided slates, and a subscription of rupees two per month. Vishnupanth Thatte, a brahmin teacher, started offering classes. Major Candy, principal at the Poona Sanskrit College, offered books.

Soon, another school was opened at Budhwar Peth, with the help of Annasaheb Chiplunkar, a brahmin. Savitribai Phule became the headmistress there.

By 1852, Savitribai Phule and Jyotirao Phule had opened three schools in Pune. These had about 150 students. But finding the money to keep them running was a massive problem. Jyotirao worked part-time in a missionary school which helped him run the house, while Savitri did not take any salary for her work as teacher and headmistress. They lived a simple life, with basic food and clothing, and their greatest joy came from the help they could offer to those in need. Their schools were open to all, but mostly, they wanted those from the most deprived parts of society to benefit from the education they provided.

Those belonging to mahar and mang castes had suffered the greatest caste discrimination, lived in poverty and were treated as social outcastes. They could not participate in events and gatherings where other castes and groups were involved. The Phules felt that education could help change this; that they should acquire a voice that had long been subdued.

So Savitribai and Jyotirao's work extended beyond the schools. They set up a mandali or institution that invited people to come and share their views on education, especially for backward groups. They formed two institutions—the Native Female School and the Society for Promoting the Education of Mahars, Mangs and Etceteras. Through these two organizations, they opened an entire network of schools in Pune.

As time went by, the schools got a reputation for providing high quality education to its students. Towards the end of October 1851, the Inspector of Schools held an inspection in one of their schools. The officer was in for a pleasant surprise. The students were knowledgeable, articulate, prompt and smart.

'These girls have been in school for such a short time. How did they turn out to be so smart?' he wondered. 'What a pity they did not get the opportunity to go to school earlier!'

The following year, the first annual examination was held for these girls. News reports of the time say that in February 1853, a huge crowd gathered to observe the remarkable event at Poona College. Two hundred and thirty-seven girls appeared for their final examinations here.

An article in the *Poona Observer* of 29 May 1852 mentioned that the students in Savitribai's schools were doing much better than those in government schools. Someone who was associated with the government schools wrote that Savitribai and Jyotirao's schools provided much better education than the government schools, and hence more girls were joining those than boys in government schools. If this continued, then the girls would eclipse the boys in no time, the writer said. 'If the Government Education Board does not do something about this soon, seeing these women outshine the men will make us hang our heads in shame,' they wrote.

This was true. When government checks in schools were done, Savitribai and Jyotirao's schools were always found to be sparkling clean. The walls were filled with creative works done by students that spoke of good moral conduct and the need to grow strong independent voices.

This showed that the schools also focused on creativity and character-building.

All the efforts of the young couple and their backbreaking work did not go unnoticed. The British government decided to felicitate Jyotirao Phule. On 16 November 1852, at a public function in Vishrambaug Wada, Jyotirao Phule was commended for his contribution to women's education.

Of course, this was criticized by those from the upper caste. It was unthinkable that a shudra could be honoured with a ceremonial shawl, they said.

# Chapter Five

In the India of the times—the 19th century—many passionate debates were happening on the education of women. There were debates on whether or not to set up schools for women. Many felt girls should go to school while others believed home schooling was good enough.

Some felt that setting up girls' schools was essential as it would free them from the purdah system. Women's education was discussed at length, not just for the poor, shudras and ati-shudras, but also as a general question for all classes and castes.

Many missionaries, and a large number of Indian men, wanted women to get an education so they could become ideal mothers, wives and companions to educated men. Many of these men were going abroad for higher education and wanted their wives to have at least some basic education.

Also up for debate was what should a woman learn. Most said they should be taught subjects that would help them become good wives and mothers and help them manage homes expertly: a bit of mathematics, needlework, moral education, some writing, and history. Music and sports were not much encouraged. Neither was the learning of English as it was a language used 'outside' the home.

All this, of course, happened over many years through the 19th century.

In her schools, Savitribai, her friends, and colleagues, taught not just lessons from books, but helped the young girls to have a mind of their own. This is evident from the writing of a young girl, Muktabai or Mukta Salve, one of Savitribai's students. Muktabai had written an essay in 1855 when she was fourteen years old and had been to school for just three years. The essay is considered a milestone in the history of Marathi and modern dalit literature.

The editor of *Dnyanodaya*, a Marathi periodical established in 1842, heard about Muktabai's piece and was bowled over by her original and powerful observations. It was published in two parts, in February and March 1855, in the periodical published from Ahmednagar. It is titled '*Mang Maharanchya*

*Dukhavisatha*' (about the grief of mahars and mangs).

In the essay, Muktabai wrote:

The brahmins have degraded us [mahars and mangs] so low, they consider people like us even lower than cows and buffaloes. Did they not consider us even lower than donkeys during the rule of Bajirao Peshwa?

*She added:* When we were punished for even passing through their doors, where was the question of getting education, getting freedom to learn? When any mang or mahar would learn somehow to read or write, and if Bajirao came to know about this, he would say: education of a mang or mahar amounts to taking away a brahmin's job.

*Her anguish is evident from these lines:* Oh, the mahars and mangs, you are poor and sick.

Only the medicine of knowledge will cure and heal you. It will take you away from wild beliefs and superstitions. You will become righteous and moral. It will stop exploitation. People who treat you like animals will not dare to treat [you] like that any more. So please work hard and study. Get educated and become good human beings.

For the teachers, it was exhilarating to see their student be recognized for her powerful words. Yet, running the schools was not always smooth sailing. Attendance was not always good, and many stopped coming. Many girls became dropouts as they got married and moved elsewhere, or their families didn't allow them to go to school anymore

'Why are they not coming back if they love school as much as they claimed?' Savitribai asked herself that question every now and then.

'Is there something wrong with our teaching method?'

'Are our lessons boring?'

'Are we failing to inspire?'

'Is the curriculum not good enough?'

'Or is there some other reason?'

'I must talk to them,' Savitribai said.

With a mission to unearth the truth, Savitribai went to the homes of a few children. Their houses were pitiably small. There were a few utensils here and there, and it seemed the families had nothing to cook for dinner. Difficulties and sorrow had etched lines on the faces of the adults.

'What is the point of going to school?' some mothers asked Savitribai.

'Who will marry them if they learn so much?'

'Can they ever become a teacher like you? Then why spoil their chances of marriage by going to school?'

'At least if they don't go to school, they can sweep the floor somewhere and earn a few coins.'

These were the responses in most homes.

Savitribai understood that in the minds of the children and parents, school was a sheer waste of time. She explained that education would get them better work, it would make them confident. They could be teachers, write books or articles in periodicals. Though options for women to work in 19th-century India were limited, learning was definitely better than remaining unlettered, she said.

'Moreover, they must protest the wrongs that shudras and ati-shudras have silently suffered for years,' Savitribai added, her voice kind and patient. 'How can they even understand they are being exploited if they don't know their own history?'

Though mild-mannered, she had the power to win arguments and influence people.

Many more meetings followed between parents, teachers and children. Savitribai understood that her students needed to learn skills that they could use in an occupation or trade. They learned painting, stitching and various other work that would help them get jobs or start their own trades. If an industrial department was attached to schools for children to learn various trades and crafts, schools would no longer be considered 'waste of time' by the poor. Jyotirao and Savitribai focused on providing girls and boys with an education that involved vocational training and was job-oriented.

Savitribai not only made the lessons interesting, she and Jyotirao also brought in the system of offering incentive money or 'salary' to the children for attending classes. The parents were moved. The reasons for going to school as explained by Savitribai seemed convincing.

'It will get them jobs.'

'School will offer little bit of money for the children (the little that we can afford).'

'It will help them choose right over wrong.'

'It will encourage creativity, and your child will be able to do something no one has done before. Give them a chance.'

'Education will teach them empathy and kindness. They will rid the world of brutality.'

'If only the brahmins send their children to school, your children will miss the opportunity and won't be able to speak for their rights.'

Not just Muktabai, all students from Savitribai's schools were inquisitive and talented. Once they got a fair chance, they grew wings and flew to reach for the stars!

Sometimes, felicitation programmes were held in schools to encourage the children with rewards for good performance. In one such programme, when a girl went up to the stage to receive her prize, she told the chief guest, 'Sir, I don't want toys as prize. We want a library for our school.'

Savitribai's heart swelled with pride, her eyes filled with tears of joy.

## *Chapter Six*

Savitri was lying on the bed, moving back and forth between sleep and wakefulness. Her back ached with fatigue, her eyelids were heavy with sleep. She had finished a long day of backbreaking work at home and in school, followed by a meeting with some children and their parents. Yet her lips twitched and she saw some images with her mind's eye every time she dozed off. Some letters were floating by, and they formed sentences. They wouldn't let her sleep.

'If I let them leave me now, I will never be able find those sentences again...' Savitribai

mumbled in her sleep. Saying this, she woke up with a start. Washing her face, she lit a lamp and sat down to write the poem.

Night after night, sometimes in the middle of the day during a break, Savitribai wrote poems. She jotted them down in her diary. In

1854, Savitribai's book of poems, *Kavya Phule* (Poetry's Blossoms), was published. Through her poems too, she spoke about the need to take education seriously.

In the poem 'Go, Get Education', she wrote:

*Be self-reliant, be industrious*
*Work, gather wisdom and riches,*
*All gets lost without knowledge*
*We become animals without wisdom...*
*You've got a golden chance to learn*
*So learn and break the chains of caste.*
*Throw away the brahmin's scriptures fast.'*

Savitribai was also in favour of shudra and ati-shudra children learning English. She believed that the English language would give them better opportunities in their lives.

*Make self-reliance your occupation,*
*Exert yourself to gather the wealth of knowledge,*
*Without knowledge animals remained dumb,*
*Don't rest! Strive to educate yourself.*
*The opportunity is here,*
*For the shudras and ati-shudras,*
*To learn English*
*To dispel all woes.*
*Throw away the authority*
*Of the brahmin and his teachings,*
*Break the shackles of caste,*
*By learning English.*

In fact, in one of her poems, she equates the English language to a deity (Mother). She believed that the knowledge of English would open new opportunities for the most deprived.

It would give them a life of dignity that they had long been denied.

*Engreji Maooli, deii satya gyan*

*Shudrala Jeevan, deii prem*

*Engreji Maooli, shudranan pana paji*

*Sangopan aaji kartes*

*Engreji Maooli todte pashutv*

*Deii manushyatv shudraloka.* (Mother English, gives true knowledge, / Rewards the lower castes with dignified life. And also affection. / It offers waters to them, as Mother does. / English destroys beastliness and awards kind-heartedness.)

*Kavya Phule* is a collection of forty-one poems and includes poems on women's rights, rights of shudras and ati-shudras, on nature and history. Savitribai poured her heart out when she wrote these bold, assertive and inspiring verses. Much later, in 1892, another collection of her poems, *Bavan Kashi Subodh Ratnakar* (The Ocean of Pure Gems) was published.

'Awake, arise and educate / Smash traditions —liberate!' is a common refrain in her poetry.

Savitribai's verses on English education show that some people had a different view about the British coming to India. For many who had been traditionally repressed, the British rulers were 'saviours' who had 'saved' them from upper-caste brutality.

Just as Savitribai encouraged the learning of the English language, her student Mukta Salve, too, wrote in her essay how the coming of the British in India had improved the lives of the lower castes.

In her renowned essay mentioned earlier, Muktabai wrote: 'The mang and mahar children never dare to lodge a complaint even if the brahmin children throw stones at them and injure them seriously. They suffer silently because they know they have to go to the brahmin's house to beg for leftover food. Alas! O God! What agony this! I will burst into tears if I write more about this injustice. Because of such oppression, the merciful God has bestowed on us this benevolent British government.'

She goes on to add: 'Harassment and torture of mahars and mangs, common during the rule of Peshwas in Pune, have stopped. Now, human sacrifice for the foundation of forts and mansions has stopped—now, nobody buries us alive. Now, our population is growing in numbers. Earlier, if any mahar or mang wore fine clothes, they would say that only brahmins should wear such clothes. Seen in fine clothes, we were earlier accused of stealing such clothes. Their religion was in danger of being polluted when untouchables put clothes around their bodies; they would tie them to trees and punish them. But, under British rule, anybody with money can buy and wear clothes.'

Muktabai also wrote that earlier, punishment for the untouchables was to behead them, which had stopped after the coming of the British. She said that 'excessive and exploitative tax' imposition (on the untouchables by the upper-caste) had also stopped and so had the practice of untouchability, in some places. 'Now, we can even visit the market place. Under the impartial

British rule, many such things have happened.' Muktabai writes that, 'Some noble souls have started schools for mahars and mangs, and such schools are supported by the merciful British government.'

These were differing views on the British rule in the country. While many fought against British imperialists, the British also helped flush out various backward, primitive and brutal practices with the help of Indian educationists and social reformers.

Even as she and her husband were running the schools, Savitribai felt the need to reach the deprived in many more ways. She started an organization for women—the Mahila Seva

Mandal in 1852—which worked for women's rights.

She would invite women from all castes and classes. They would come to listen to her inspiring words. Savitribai Phule, simple and calm from outside, was fiery inside.

'Kaku! Mavashi!' she welcomed, and led her guests to a simple mat spread on the floor. This mat was meant for all. There were no separate seating arrangements on the basis of caste. With this, Savitribai wanted to establish that all had the same place in Mahila Seva Mandal.

Sitting there, listening to her inspiring words, many women understood that they had been denied education because of their gender. They felt cheated and deprived.

In the company of women from shudra and

ati-shudra caste groups, upper caste women realized how divisions based on caste and gender were used to control and oppress. Shudra and ati-shudra women faced this bias doubly because of their caste identity.

As Savitribai, Fatima Sheikh and many others like them narrated stories and anecdotes to explain their rights, the women sat there listening intently. They faced brutal torture at home from their husbands, there were horror stories of how some women's noses were cut off as punishment. Such violence should stop, they felt.

Education for women was the only answer, they agreed. They promised to send their daughters to school, and pledged to not bow down before others. They wanted an equal society. Back home, not all were able to send their daughters to school, not all were forthright enough to demand formal education for themselves, and it would take many more years for major, significant changes to be brought about in women's education and equality in India. But these were the initial years and Savitribai Phule was a trailblazer, a pioneer who was among the first to sow the seeds of change. Her efforts, by using the tools of modern Western/English education, furthered the cause of equality and created allies towards social justice.

# Chapter Seven

The sixteen-year-old girl sat quietly, tears streaming down her eyes. The bangles on her arms had been broken, and the vermillion mark on her forehead rubbed out by the women of the family. Now, a barber was shaving her head. Her long, black hair that reached her waist lay in clumps on the floor. Her mother had lovingly once oiled and plaited this hair. She had grumbled about this hair because it needed so much attention. But now that the barber's blade scraped at her scalp, the tears would not stop.

She had just become a widow and this was the keshavapan ceremony.

Savitribai Phule was one of the first to protest this outrageous ritual along with some other social reformers. Narayan Meghaji Lokhande was one of the members of the Satyashodhak Samaj that was formed by Jyotirao Phule. He, Jyotirao Phule and Savitribai Phule urged and organized members of the barbers community to boycott the tonsuring of widows in order to do away with the cruel practice. It was a significant event that took place in 1890 and was reported in newspapers.

But well before that, Savitribai and Jyotiba had started their work for widows. As soon as a woman lost her husband, her head would be tonsured, and she would be made to wear white clothes for the rest of her life. Without money or property, widows were totally at the mercy of their male relatives. They were brutally exploited by men within the family, and by neighbours and acquaintances. Widowhood meant a lifetime of ill treatment and discrimination.

Did the shastras, Hindu texts, really talk of keshavapan ceremony? Could a religion ask of such brutal treatment of widows? Should these practices against widows not be banned?

In the 1840s and '50s, these questions were being raised and widow remarriage became a subject of great debate. Imagine the sufferings of girls as little as nine or ten years old, who were forced to get married, and once their husbands died, they had nowhere to go! They had never gone to school, and faced torture in the hands of their relatives all their lives.

In today's time, it is unthinkable, but at that time, this was the reality for thousands of women in India.

> Educator and social reformer, Ishwar Chandra Vidyasagar, arranged the first widow remarriage in India on 7 December 1856, in Kolkata (then Calcutta), West Bengal. The woman, Kalimati, daughter of Brahmananda Mukherjee, was married to Shrishchandra Vidyaratna in the house of Raj Krishna Bandyopadhyay. The Hindu Widows' Remarriage Act 1856, legalised the remarriage of widows in India. It followed a long campaign led by Vidyasagar to do away with the sufferings of widows, a large number of whom were children and adolescent girls. He faced severe opposition from Hindu society.

Bit by bit, Indian women began to fight for the rights of child widows, and even asked that the British government bring in laws on this. 'Keshavapan has no religious basis, and had been created by men to control women,' they said.

These arguments came in gradually, but Savitribai Phule was among the first women in the country who thought of ways to support widows and stop their exploitation. One way to do this was by providing safehouses and shelters where a woman who had been abused by a man could leave her baby.

When a widow was abused by a man and she was going to have a baby, the man, in most cases, refused to take care of her and the baby. This drove the women to shame. Instead of blaming the abuser, people blamed the women.

One such case was the incident of a young brahmin widow, Kashibai. When Kashibai gave birth to a child, the man would not take any responsibility of the baby. Fearing the shame that would be heaped on her, Kashibai killed the child and threw the body in a well. When the body was found, she was arrested and sentenced to life imprisonment in the Andamans, in 1863. It was possibly the first time a woman had been sentenced to such severe imprisonment.

This news upset Savitribai and Jyotirao.

Savitribai could not imagine standing by when women around her suffered so terribly. Together, they decided to set up a shelter home for widows in their own home at Ganj Peth, Pune. It came to be known as the 'Balhatya Pratibandhak Griha' (Home for the Prevention of Infanticide).

Savitribai, Jyotirao and his friend Sadashiv Ballal Govande started the centre.

Word spread, but to make sure more people knew about it, they put up posters and pamphlets in various parts of the town. 'Widows, come here and deliver your baby safely and secretly. It is up to your discretion whether you want to keep the baby in the centre or take it with you. This orphanage will take care of the children [left behind].': this is what the posters said. Many went there and started living in the home. By the 1880s, there were thirty-five widows who had come from various places to live at the shelter home. Savitribai would help in the delivery of the babies and take care of them.

# Chapter Eight

Savitribai was worried about the ever increasing expenses. But she was gritty, firm, feisty, yet impressed everyone with her simplicity. She would never express anger or exasperation. From the outside, no one could make out that she was under stress.

Very often, a needy person would knock at their door looking for the kind lady Savitribai.

'The poor woman has not eaten for days!' Savitribai would rummage through her kitchen and find some raw vegetables and grains of rice. After some pondering, she would take some boiled rice on a plate and some cooked vegetables to feed the guest. 'She needs to eat right away. God knows when was the last time she had some food!' she would tell Jyotirao, who would pretend to read a book, but actually watch Savitribai from the corner of his eyes, amused.

While the needy woman waited in the courtyard, Savitribai would take one of her sarees, and a few coins.

'Kaku, take these. Take care of your health. Buy some milk and sugar, you are hardly able to walk,' she would say.

Jyotirao would watch Savitribai with a twinkle in his eyes, and a little smile would play in the corner of his lips. 'One must not spend so much! We are unable to bear the expenses of our homes and schools already,' he would say.

'I am aware of that. We will manage somehow. In any case, what are we going to take away with us when we die?' she would reply, smiling.

And Jyotirao, who couldn't agree more, wouldn't have anything to say to that after all!

Social reform was happening in various parts of the country at the time, led by different sections of the people. A number of organizations had been led by brahmin social reformers. Those like the Brahmo Samaj (formed in 1828), Arya Samaj (formed in 1875), wanted to improve society by helping others. Savitribai and Jyotirao felt that though these organizations wanted to bring social reforms, none of them looked specifically at the interests of the most downtrodden—the shudras and ati-shudras.

With this thought was born the Satyashodhak Samaj, set up by Jyotirao Phule, Savitribai and their other like-minded friends on 24 September 1873. Satyashodhak means 'Seekers of the Truth'. The Satyashodhak Samaj called for the coming together of all castes (including women) to fight brahmin domination. They wanted to fight in various ways for equal opportunities in education, jobs, social prestige, etc. They wanted recognition for the work they did, respect and equality. While shudras and ati-shudras often did the most difficult jobs, the credit or recognition was never there for them.

The Satyashodhak Samaj was the beginning of a non-brahmin movement in western India. One very important step taken by the organization was to introduce a new kind of marriage by giving up old rituals and customs. Upper-caste marriages were full of pomp and show of clothes, jewellery, with lavish feasts and dowry. This was unacceptable to social reformers, who were disgusted by such opulence when so many people were hungry and deprived.

The Samaj gave up the traditional system and introduced marriages that were performed without a brahmin priest and without brahminical rituals. It adopted modern and liberal marriage ceremonies. Jyotirao Phule and other members of the Samaj wrote 'alternative verses' for it. The bride and groom sang the verses, in the presence of their family, friends and other guests. The groom pledged to work for equal rights of women, and the couple took an oath to take care of each other. Satyashodhak marriages were simple, with minimum expense and no dowry.

The first Satyashodhak marriage took place on 25 December 1873, between activist Sitaram Jabaji Alhat and Radha Nimbankar. Radha was the daughter of Savitribai's friend. The movement spread far and wide, and such marriages have continued to take place over the years.

By not allowing the brahmins to preside over their weddings, the Satyashodhak Samaj, through its unique wedding rituals, was actually challenging their authority. A number of cases were filed in courts against this kind of marriage for not involving the brahmins, as it had directly affected their source of livelihood.

> In the 1920s, a similar form of marriage took place in India as part of the Self Respect Movement (headed by social reformer Periyar). Self-respect marriages (known as *tanmaanam* or *suya mariyadai*, meaning 'self-respect') took place without the supervision of brahmin priests. Though this movement was led in Tamil Nadu, it became very popular among Tamils even outside India.

Savitribai and Jyotirao faced criticism not just because of the work they did for others, but also for their personal lives.

'Why don't you have a child of your own?'

'It must be the woman's fault.'

'She can't be a good mother because she has no interest in household duties. She is reading books and working outside the home. God must have punished her and not given her a child.'

'Why doesn't he marry another woman? Who will conduct his last rites when he dies if he does not have a son?'

These were the questions raised by people all around them. Some of them said mean things about Savitribai. They were afraid of Jyotirao, as he was a *man*, even though he was simple and meek. But some friends, relatives and colleagues did raise the matter with him, and suggested that he should marry a second time. The usually calm Jyotirao was furious when he was offered such unsolicited advice. 'If the fault lies with the man and not the woman, are women advised to marry a second time?' he asked. 'Will it be acceptable to you if women marry again and bring another man home?'

Since Jyotirao and Savitri both wanted a child, in 1873, they adopted a child from the infanticide prevention centre that they ran. They named him Yashwant.

Yashwant was a mischievous little thing and Savitribai and Jyotiba doted on him. He was given immense love and was taught the true value of education by his parents. Under the guidance of these two outstanding human beings, he would grow up to be a sensitive and responsible young man.

In July 1887, Jyotirao suffered a stroke which left him paralyzed and bedridden for several months. But as soon as his condition improved, he would sit on the bed and keep writing, planning and working. Savitribai looked at him in awe. She was happy she had been married to someone who refused to rest, and believed in

working all the time. By now, they both felt that it was time for Yashwant to be married.

They chose a girl named Radha (also called Laxmi). She was the daughter of Satyashodhak Samaj leader Gyanoba Krishnaji Sasane. Savitribai asked Radha to live in the Phule home before she and Yashwant were married. 'She must feel comfortable with us. If she does not like being here, how will she feel once she has been married to Yashwant?' Savitribai told Jyotiba. 'We must know what she likes and dislikes and so should she.'

On 4 February 1889, at the age of sixteen, Yashwant got married to Radha following the Satyashodhak system. It was perhaps the first inter-caste marriage in modern India. As the bride and the groom chanted the mangalashtak (mantras), they pledged to be caring and respectful to each other. Savitribai made sure that Radha continued with her education after marriage. It is said that she ensured that her daughter-in-law got enough rest so she could study more and not get saddled with housework.

In 1877, when a severe drought hit Maharashtra, Savitribai and Jyotirao went to villages and towns collecting funds and started the Victoria Balashram in Dhankawadi. Their friends came out to support them too. At the centre, one thousand poor persons were offered food every day. Savitribai would cook the food herself along with her friends. They also ran a hostel at the centre, where students could come and stay.

After Jyotirao's stroke, though he recovered and started his work again, he could not be as active as he was earlier. The family and their projects started suffering as the expenses were huge compared to the donations they were receiving for their centres, schools and trusts.

On 28 November 1890, Jyotirao passed away.

His lifelong friend and companion, Savitribai, mourned for him.

In some regions of India, among Hindus, whoever holds the titve (earthen pot) during the cremation is considered the 'successor' of the deceased person and can claim rights over his property. During Jyotirao's cremation, his nephew wanted to hold the titve denying Yashwant the right, as he was an adopted son.

At this point, Savitribai told everyone that she wanted to hold the titve herself. And so she did, leading the people at the cremation. She was possibly the first woman in India to perform the last rites of a husband. Such rites are assigned only to male children, and by carrying out this ritual at a time when no one could even imagine it possible, Savitribai proved yet another time that she was an extraordinary and brave woman who believed in following her heart.

After Jyotirao Phule's death, Savitribai led the Satyashodhak movement, and was the chairperson of the Satyashodhak Conference held in 1893 in Pune's Saswad. It was remarkable for a woman to lead the conference.

Yashwant's wife Radha passed away in 1895. Savitribai was heartbroken. With grief in her heart, she continued to work. 'It is only through serving people that I can forget my personal grief,' she told herself.

She woke up early in the morning as usual, bathed, cooked, ate a bit and left for work for the whole day. She cooked for others, helped feed the distressed, the students, and held meetings to arrange for funds and spoke to women and men who needed support. The day went by in a flash. But at the end of a long and tiring day, she dropped to her bed and wept, missing Jyotirao and Radha.

Savitribai was aging, but she kept working during every calamity and difficulty. Thus, when there was a drought in 1896, and in 1897 there was the bubonic plague, she kept working for the poor.

Hundreds of people were dying in Pune from the plague. Savitribai worked hard to ensure they got treatment, and a temporary hospital was set up in the fields. She knew no fear and was not afraid of anything, not even a deadly disease, when it came to helping others. She would hold the sick, pick them up and take them to the hospital. She sat for hours by their side when doctors offered treatment. She fed them, she said kind words to make them feel better.

Bubonic plague is a highly contagious disease, and it was no surprise that Savitribai herself was afflicted. On 10 March 1897, Savitribai Phule passed away. She was sixty-six years old.

Her whole life, Savitribai always led from the front. Every single time, she took the unchartered paths that no one else one had dared to take before. She was fearless, and faced criticisms and worse with calm bravery. She turned customs, rituals and beliefs on their head if they were unkind and oppressed the weak. Savitribai Phule always did what came to her naturally by following her instincts and listening to her inner voice. Not only in life, even in her death, she showed how thoughtful she was about the poor and the sick. For over fifty years, Savitribai Phule dedicated her life wholeheartedly for the welfare of people.

Savitribai Phule is remembered for the pioneering work she did to improve the condition of shudras, ati-shudras and women at a time when they were the most deprived and ill-treated in society. Following the path that she had created, many schools for girls, especially for the most underprivileged girls, were set up across the country over the next few decades. Not only schools, she implemented new ideas in every sphere of life, leading by example and asking women to demand equal rights.

At the root of her work were simple concepts—that education could bring happiness and power to individuals by making them free, independent and self-sufficient, and the need to treat all humans on equal footing. She was calm as well as an iron-willed leader, a trailblazer who preached equality for all, beyond class, caste and gender divisions. She opened schools for girls, offered food and shelter to ostracized widows and their children, and to those affected by floods and plague. Most significantly, she practised in her own life the changes she worked hard to bring about in society.

# *Savitribai Phule*
## *A Timeline*

- 3 January 1831: Savitribai Phule born in Naigaon in Maharashtra's Satara.
- 1840: Savitribai is married to Jyotirao Phule.
- 1848: They start a school, which becomes the first school for girls in the country to be opened by Indians.
- 1849: Faced with opposition, Jyotiba Phule's father asks him and Savitribai to leave his house.
- By 1852: Savitribai and Jyotirao Phule start the first three schools.

- 1854: Savitribai publishes *Kavya Phule*, her first collection of poems in Marathi.
- 1863: Balhatya Pratibandhak Griha (Home for the Prevention of Infanticide) is formed.
- 1863: Savitribai and Jyotirao adopt a child. They name him Yashwant.
- 24 September 1873: Satyashodhak Samaj (Seekers of the Truth organization) is set up by Jyotirao Phule along with Savitribai and other friends.
- 4 February 1889: Yashwant and Radha get married following the Satyashodhak system, in what was perhaps the first inter-caste marriage in modern India.
- 1890: Jyotiba Phule passes away.
- 1893: Savitribai Phule is the chairperson of the Satyadhodhak Conference in Pune's Saswad.

- 1897: Savitribai helps patients during the plague epidemic.
- 10 March 1897: Savitribai Phule passes away after becoming afflicted by plague while taking care of plague patients.

# Author's Note

Sometimes I wonder whether Savitribai and Jyotiba Phule would have achieved what they did had they not been married to each other. This is not a frivolous thought, but a way of understanding how real 'progress' can take place if women and men encourage and support each other in their endeavours. Every young person should draw inspiration from the story of Savitribai Phule, and also aspire to be like Jyotiba who found joy in being his partner's equal, not superior.

My main sources of information were the essay 'Dnyanajyoti Savitribai Phule', by Prof. Hari Narake, published by National Council of Educational Research and Training (NCERT), 2009; *Women's Consciousness and Assertion in Colonial India: Gender, Social Reform and Politics in Maharashtra C. 1870- C. 1920*, by Padma Anagol-McGinn, School of Oriental and African Studies, University of London, 1994; *Caste Matters* by Suraj Yengde, Penguin Books, 2019; *Women Writing In India, 600 B.C. to the Present*, edited by Susie Tharu & K. Lalita, Oxford University Press, 1991. Mukta Salve's letter in English has been quoted from dalitweb.org.

Also used as references were Tejas Harad's piece, 'Remembering Jotiba Phule, the Mahatma

Who Fought Against Brahmin Hegemony', published in newslaundry.com, (that mentions Shriram Gundekar's book *Maharashtrache Shilpkar: Mahatma Jyotiba Phule* as a source); Sanjoy Chakravorty's piece in bbc.com titled 'How the British Reshaped India's Caste System' and Divya Kandukuri's piece in *The Mint*, titled 'The Life and Times of Savitribai Phule'.

Dates on various events in Savitribai Phule's life vary among these sources. Such things do happen due to lack of records and their availability. However, it's the impact of these events and their significance that counts more.

Savitribai Phule's poems have been taken from these sources: 'Make self-reliance your occupation...' has been taken from the Savitribai Phule First Memorial Lecture publication containing Prof. Hari Narake's essay mentioned above, in which MG Mali's collection of Savitribai Phule's writings has been referred to. The poem *'Engreji Maooli'* has been taken from a piece by Awanish Somkuwar published in dailypioneer.com (*The Pioneer*). The poems 'Go, Get Education' and 'Awake, Arise and Educate' are taken from a piece by Shivani Waldekar in feminisminindia.com, that references MG Mali's *Krantijyoti Savitribai Jyotirao Phule*, Asha Prakashan, Gargoti, 1980 and MG Mali, *Savitribai Phule, Samagra Vangamaya*, Maharashtra Rajya Sahitya Mandal, Mumbai, 2006, apart from Prof. Hari Narake's essay. My sincere gratitude to all.

I am grateful to Dr Maroona Murmu, Professor, Department of History, Jadavpur University and Sounak Roy, dalit scholar, for agreeing to do an incisive reading of the manuscript. Sounak Roy's valuable suggestions for narrating Savitribai Phule's story as a story of caste/class subjugation have been enriching for this book as well as for me as an individual. My love and gratitude to Riju Basu for his generosity and support.

Swati Sengupta